~A BINGO BOOK~

Around The World Bingo Book

COMPLETE BINGO GAME IN A BOOK

Written By Rebecca Stark

ISBN 978-0-87386-468-8

Educational Books 'n' Bingo

Printed in the U.S.A.

AROUND THE WORLD BINGO DIRECTIONS

INCLUDED:

List of Terms

Templates for Additional Terms and Clues

2 Clues per Term

30 Unique Bingo Cards

Markers

1. **Either cut apart the book or make copies of ALL the sheets. You might want to make an extra copy of the clue sheets to use for introduction and review. Keep the sheets in an envelope for easy reuse.**

2. Cut apart the call cards with terms and clues.

3. Pass out one bingo card per student. There are enough for a class of 30.

4. Pass out markers. You may cut apart the markers included in this book or use any other small items of your choice.

5. Decide whether or not you will require the entire card to be filled. Requiring the entire card to be filled provides a better review. However, if you have a short time to fill, you may prefer to have them do the just the border or some other format. Tell the class before you begin what is required.

6. There are 50 terms. Read the list before you begin. If there are any terms that have not been covered in class, you may want to read to the students the term and clues before you begin.

7. There is a blank space in the middle of each card. You can instruct the students to use it as a free space or you can write in answers to cover terms not included. Of course, in this case you would create your own clues. (Templates provided.)

8. Shuffle the cards and place them in a pile. Two or three clues are provided for each term. If you plan to play the game with the same group more than once, you might want to choose a different clue for each game. If not, you may choose to use more than one clue.

9. Be sure to keep the cards you have used for the present game in a separate pile. When a student calls, "Bingo," he or she will have to verify that the correct answers are on his or her card AND that the markers were placed in response to the proper questions. Pull out the cards that are on the student's card keeping them in the order they were used in the game. Read each clue as it was given and ask the student to identify the correct answer from his or her card.

10. If the student has the correct answers on the card AND has shown that they were marked in response to the *correct questions,* then that student is the winner and the game is over. If the student does not have the correct answers on the card OR he or she marked the answers in response to *the wrong questions,* then the game continues until there is a proper winner.

11. If you want to play again, reshuffle the cards and begin again.

Have fun!

PLACES

OCEANS:

The Arctic Ocean

The Atlantic Ocean

The Indian Ocean

The Pacific Ocean

The Southern (Antarctic) Ocean

CONTINENTS:

Africa

Antarctica

Asia

Australia / Oceania

Europe

North America

South America

COUNTRIES:

Algeria

Argentina

Austria

Brazil

Canada

People's Republic of China

Colombia

Croatia

Czech Republic

Democratic Republic of the Congo

Denmark

Egypt

England

Ethiopia

France

Germany

Greece

Iraq

India

Ireland

Israel

Italy

Japan

Kenya

Mexico

The Netherlands

New Zealand

Poland

The Russian Federation

South Africa

South Korea

Spain

Switzerland

Syria

Turkey

United States

Venezuela

Vietnam

Additional Terms

Choose as many additional places or terms as you would like and write them in the squares. Repeat each as desired.
Cut out the squares and randomly distribute them to the class.
Instruct the students to place their square on the center space of their card.

Around the World Bingo

Clues for Additional Terms

Write three clues for each of your additional terms.

_____

1.

2.

3.

_____

1.

2.

3.

_____

1.

2.

3.

_____

1.

2.

3.

_____

1.

2.

3.

_____

1.

2.

3.

© **Barbara M. Peller**

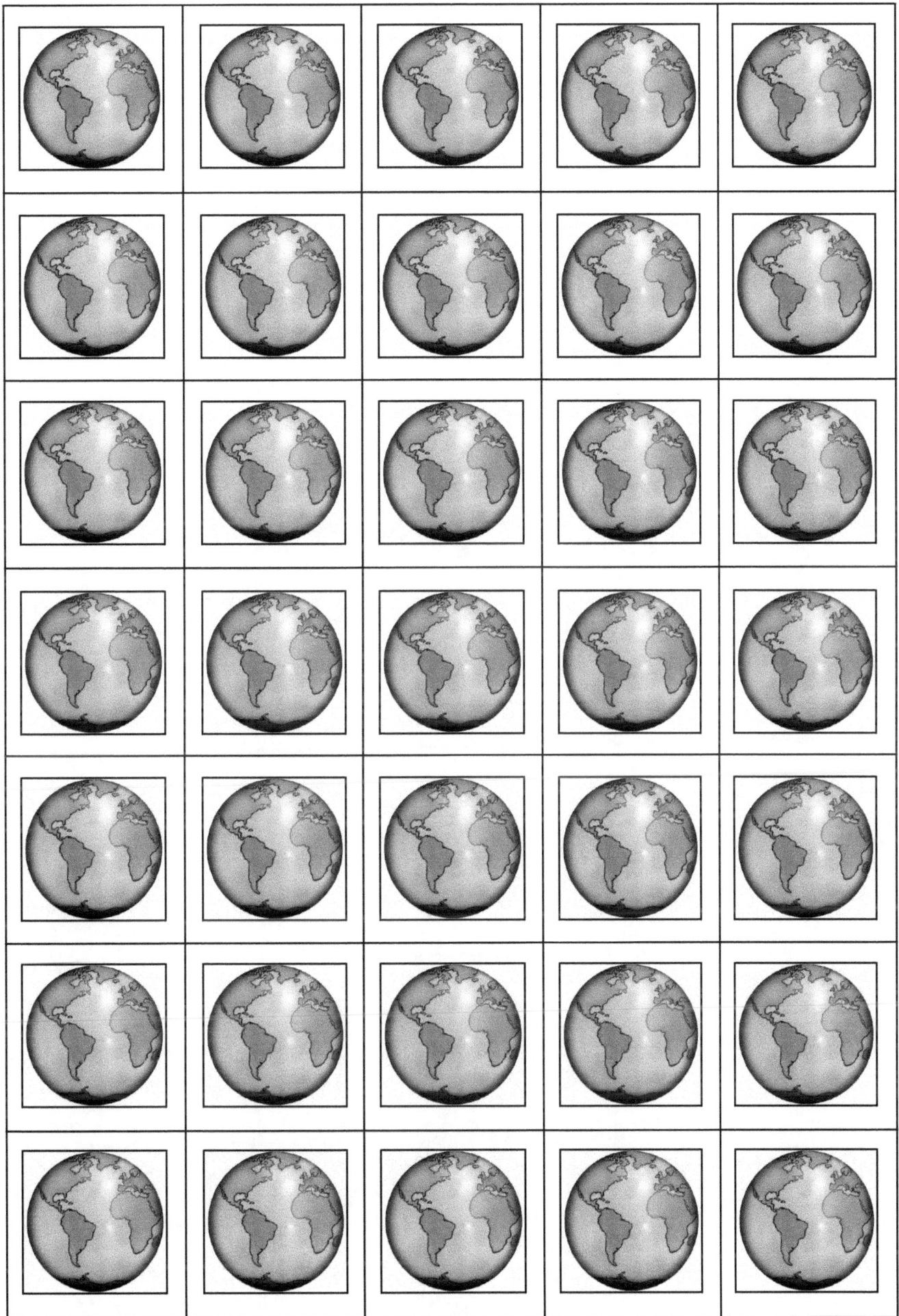

THE ARCTIC OCEAN	THE ATLANTIC OCEAN
1. It is Earth's smallest ocean. 2. Lomonosov Ridge divides this ocean into two basins: the Eurasian Basin and the North American Basin. 3. Its central surface is covered by a perennial, drifting polar icepack.	1. It is the second largest ocean but it is relatively shallow. 2. It is the eastern border of the United States. 3. The Sargasso Sea is an elongated region in the middle of this ocean,
THE INDIAN OCEAN	**THE PACIFIC OCEAN**
1. This ocean is located between Africa, the Southern Ocean, Asia and Australia. 2. A devastating tsunami in this ocean hit the west coast of Sumatra, Indonesia, South and Southeast Asia, Sri Lanka, India and Thailand in 2004. 3. It is the third largest ocean.	1. This is the largest, deepest and oldest of the five oceans. 2. This ocean is bordered by North and South America on the east and Asia and Australia on the west. 3. Its basin is known as the "Ring of Fire."
THE SOUTHERN OCEAN	**AFRICA**
1. This ocean used to be considered the southern regions of the Atlantic, Pacific and Indian oceans. 2. In 2000 the International Hydrographic Organization declared it to be the fifth ocean. 3. It is the only place on Earth where water encircles the entire globe.	1. It is the world's second-largest and second most-populous continent. 2. This continent comprises 46 countries including the island nation Madagascar and 53 countries if all the island groups are included. 3. The largest country in this continent is Sudan; the smallest is the Seychelles.
ANTARCTICA	**ASIA**
1. It is Earth's southernmost continent. 2. There are no permanent human residents on this continent. 3. A treaty signed by 45 countries (as of this date) prohibits military activities and mineral mining to protect this continent's ecosystems.	1. It is the world's largest and most populous continent. 2. Some geographers do not consider this and Europe to be separate continents because there is no logical physical separation between them. 3. Japan is located in this continent.
AUSTRALIA / OCEANIA	**EUROPE**
1. The Great Barrier Reef can be found off the coast of this continent. 2. It is the smallest and lowest-lying continent. 3. The mainland of this continent is a country of the same name.	1. It is the sixth largest continent. 2. This continent is separated from Asia by Russia's Ural Mountains and the Caspian and Black seas. 3. Many countries of this continent formed an economic union; their unit of currency is the euro.

Around the World Bingo

© Barbara M. Peller

NORTH AMERICA	SOUTH AMERICA
1. It is the third largest continent in size and is located in the northern and western hemispheres. 2. The United States, Canada and Mexico are located in this continent. 3. The highest point on this continent is Mt. McKinley in Alaska.	1. This continent lies in the Western Hemisphere and mostly in the Southern Hemisphere. 2. The largest country in this continent in both area and population is Brazil. 3. Most people living in this continent speak either Portuguese or Spanish.
ALGERIA	**ARGENTINA**
1. Its capital and largest city is Algiers. 2. This country is bordered by Tunisia in the northeast, Libya in the east and Niger in the southeast. 3. This African country is bordered by Mali and Mauritania in the southwest.	1. Its capital and largest city is Buenos Aires. 2. The fertile plains in the center of this country are known as Las Pampas. 3. This country is known for a dance called the tango.
AUSTRIA	**BRAZIL**
1. Vienna is its capital city. 2. It borders Germany and the Czech Republic to the north, Slovakia and Hungary to the east, Slovenia and Italy to the south, and Switzerland and Liechtenstein to the west. 3. Salzburg, its fourth-largest city, was the birthplace of Wolfgang Amadeus Mozart.	1. It is the largest country in South America. 2. Its capital is Rio de Janeiro. 3. The people in this South American country speak Portuguese.
CANADA	**PEOPLE'S REPUBLIC OF CHINA**
1. Its capital is Ottawa, but its largest city is Toronto. 2. This North American country is the world's second largest country by total area. 3. The official languages of this North American country are English and French.	1. It capital city is Beijing. 2. The Great Wall in this country stretches over approximately 4,000 miles (6,400 km). 3. Shanghai is its largest city.
COLOMBIA	**REPUBLIC OF CROATIA**
1. Its capital city is Bogotá. 2. This South American country is bordered by these countries: Venezuela, Brazil, Ecuador, Peru and Panama. 3. This South American country is bordered by these bodies of water: the Atlantic Ocean, the Caribbean Sea; and the Pacific Ocean.	1. Its capital and largest city is Zagreb. A popular city for tourism is Dubrovnik. 2. This country borders on Slovenia, Hungary, Serbia, Bosnia, Herzegovina, and Montenegro. 3. This country fought for independence from Yugoslavia from 1991 until 1995, when it gained independence.

Around the World Bingo

© Barbara M. Peller

CZECH REPUBLIC
1. The capital and largest city of this country of Central Europe is Prague.
2. This country shares borders with Poland, Germany, Austria, and Slovakia.
3. The Vltava is its longest river.

DEMOCRATIC REPUBLIC OF THE CONGO
1. The capital and largest city of this African nation is Kinshasa.
2. Before gaining independence from Belgium, this country was known as the Belgian Congo.
3. In 1971 President Mobutu named the country Zaire, but it was again given its present name in 1997 after Mobutu was overthrown.

DENMARK
1. The capital and largest city of this Scandinavian country is Copenhagen.
2. It is the southernmost of the Nordic countries.
3. Author Hans Christian Andersen, famous for *The Little Mermaid* and other fairy tales, was born in this country.

EGYPT
1. The capital and largest city of this country in North Africa is Cairo.
2. Most of the people in this country of North Africa live near the banks of the Nile River.
3. Karnak Temple and the Valley of the Kings are located in the southern city of Luxor in this country.

ENGLAND
1. Its capital and largest city is London.
2. It is the most populous country of the United Kingdom of Great Britain and Northern Ireland.
3. This country takes its name from the Angles, Germanic-speaking people who settled there during the 5th and 6th centuries.

ETHIOPIA
1. Addis Ababa is its capital and largest city.
2. This landlocked country is bordered by Eritrea, Sudan, Kenya, Somalia and Djibouti.
3. Emperor Haile Selassie I reigned during the early twentieth century.

FRANCE
1. Its capital and largest city is Paris.
2. Its name comes from a Latin word which means "land of the Franks."
3. Its rivers include the Loire, the Garonne, the Seine and the Rhône.

GERMANY
1. The capital and largest city is Berlin.
2. After World War II, this country in Central Europe was divided into two separate states but was reunified in 1990.
3. This country shares borders with many countries: Denmark, Poland, the Czech Republic, Austria, Switzerland, France, Luxembourg, Belgium, and the Netherlands.

GREECE
1. Its capital and largest city is Athens.
2. In ancient times people worshiped the Olympian gods.
3. A few of the many important tourist sites are the Acropolis of Athens, the Temple of Epicurean Apollo, and the archaeological sites at Delphi and Epidaurus.

IRAQ
1. Its capital and largest city is Baghdad.
2. This country borders Kuwait, Saudi Arabia, Jordan, Syria, Turkey, and Iran.
3. In ancient times the area was known as Mesopotamia.

Around the World Bingo

INDIA	**REPUBLIC OF IRELAND**
1. Although its capital is New Delhi, its largest city is Mumbai. 2. It is the second most populous country in the world; only the People's Republic of China has a larger population. 3. Two rivers include the Ganges and the Brahmaputra, both of which drain into the Bay of Bengal.	1. Its capital and largest city is Dublin. 2. A few of its 26 counties are Limerick, Cork, Kerry and Galway. 3. The longest river of this "Emerald Isle" is the River Shannon.
ISRAEL	**ITALY**
1. Sites in Jerusalem in this nation are considered sacred by Jews, Christians and Muslims. 2. This country, which is slightly smaller than New Jersey, borders Egypt, the Gaza Strip, Jordan, Lebanon, Syria and the West Bank. 3. Tel Aviv and Haifa are two important cities.	1. Its capital and largest city is Rome. 2. Milan, Florence and Venice are three important cities. 3. The Po, this country's principal river, flows from the Alps to the Adriatic Sea.
JAPAN	**KENYA**
1. Tokyo is the capital and largest city. The name Tokyo literally means eastern capital. 2. Some other important cities are Yokohama, Osaka, Nagoya, Kobe, Hiroshima, Sapporo, and Kawasaki. 3. Mt. Fuji, a beautiful, conical peak, is this country's highest mountain.	1. Its capital and largest city is Nairobi. 2. This country is bordered by Ethiopia, Somalia, Tanzania, Uganda, and Sudan; the Indian Ocean is on the southeast border. 3. The area used to be called British East Africa.
NEW ZEALAND	**THE NETHERLANDS**
1. Its capital city is Wellington, but the largest city is Auckland. 2. This country in the southwestern Pacific Ocean comprises two large islands—the North Island and the South Island—and several smaller islands. 3. This country is separated from Australia by the Tasman Sea.	1. The capital and largest city of this country is Amsterdam. 2. The official language of this country is Dutch. 3. Rotterdam is its second-largest city and The Hague is its third-largest city.
Boston Tea Party	**POLAND**
1. The political protest known as the ___ was organized by the Sons of Liberty. It took place on December 16, 1773. 2. At the time, the ___ was usually called "the destruction of the tea."	1. The capital and largest city is Warsaw. 2. The two longest rivers of this Central European country are the Vistula and the Oder. 3. This country is bordered Germany, the Czech Republic, Slovakia, Ukraine, Belarus and Lithuania.

Around the World Bingo

THE RUSSIAN FEDERATION 1. Its capital and largest city is Moscow. 2. At 17,075,400 square kilometers (6,592,800 sq mi), it is the largest country in the world. 3. Lake Baikal in this country is the deepest lake in the world and the largest freshwater lake in the world by volume.	**SOUTH AFRICA** 1. This country has 3 capitals: Pretoria, the executive capital; Bloemfontein, the judicial capital; and Cape Town, the legislative capital. 2. The largest and most populous city in this country is Johannesburg. 3. The term "Rainbow Nation" was used to describe the country's multicultural diversity after apartheid was abolished here.
SOUTH KOREA (Republic of Korea) 1. Its capital and largest city is Seoul. 2. After Japan and China, this country has the highest gross domestic product in Asia. 3. Busan City, also known as Pusan, is the largest port and the second largest metropolis in this country.	**SPAIN** 1. Its capital and largest city is Madrid. 2. Barcelona is its second largest city and one of Europe's principal Mediterranean ports. 3. With Portugal it makes up the Iberian Peninsula.
SWITZERLAND (Swiss Confederation) 1. Its capital is Berne, but its largest city is Zurich. 2. This Western European country is a federal republic comprising 26 states, which are called cantons. 3. Geneva, its second most populous city, is surrounded by two mountain chains, the Alps and the Jura.	**SYRIA** 1. Its capital and largest city is Damascus. 2. Its name derives from the name the ancient Greeks used to refer to the Assyrians. 3. Its capital, Damascus, is one of the oldest continuously inhabited cities in the world.
TURKEY (Republic of Turkey) 1. The capital of this Eurasian country is Ankara, but its largest city is Istanbul. 2. The first known name of its most important city, Istanbul, was Byzantium. It later became known as Constantinople. 3. Its political system was established following the fall of the Ottoman Empire after World War I.	**UNITED STATES** 1. Its capital is Washington, DC, but New York City is its largest city. 2. This North American country was founded by thirteen British colonies. 3. The Hudson and the Mississippi are two important rivers in this country.
VENEZUELA (Bolivarian Republic of Venezuela) 1. Its capital and largest city is Caracas. 2. Angel Falls, the world's highest waterfall, is located in this South American country. 3. The Orinoco is the largest and most important river system of this country.	**VIETNAM (Socialist Republic of Vietnam)** 1. Its capital city is Hanoi, but its largest city is Ho Chi Minh City. 2. A war was fought in this country between the north and the south; it began in1956 and ended in 1975. 3. Its largest city, Ho Chi Minh City, was once known as Saigon.

Around the World Bingo

Around the World Bingo

The Arctic Ocean	Africa	Asia	Brazil	Democratic Republic of the Congo
Czech Republic	Egypt	New Zealand	The Indian Ocean	North America
Kenya	Colombia		England	The United States
South Korea	Switzerland	People's Republic of China	Poland	Spain
Croatia	South America	Greece	Iraq	The Russian Federation

Around the World Bingo: Card No. 1

Around the World Bingo

The Atlantic Ocean	Algeria	Denmark	France	Europe
Italy	Asia	Antarctica	Mexico	Kenya
Ethiopia	The Pacific Ocean		Syria	Austria
Israel	Vietnam	The Russian Federation	Japan	Ireland
South America	Croatia	Australia/ Oceania	Canada	Democratic Republic of the Congo

Around the World Bingo

The Southern (Antarctic) Ocean	Asia	Argentina	Venezuela	Kenya
South America	The Arctic Ocean	The Netherlands	New Zealand	Turkey
Germany	Poland		India	Africa
People's Republic of China	Brazil	Canada	Vietnam	Denmark
Europe	France	Australia/ Oceania	South Africa	Italy

Around the World Bingo: Card No. 3

Around the World Bingo

The Atlantic Ocean	The Indian Ocean	Africa	Austria	Brazil
North America	Iraq	Czech Republic	South Korea	Greece
Israel	Mexico		Spain	Turkey
England	Colombia	Ethiopia	Croatia	India
The United States	Venezuela	Ireland	Syria	Egypt

Around the World Bingo

Democratic Republic of the Congo	Germany	Denmark	Mexico	Austria
The Pacific Ocean	Antarctica	Japan	Croatia	Algeria
Vietnam	The Southern (Antarctic) Ocean		Greece	India
Czech Republic	Turkey	North America	Europe	Venezuela
New Zealand	Colombia	The Netherlands	The Russian Federation	Egypt

Around the World Bingo

The Indian Ocean	Democratic Republic of the Congo	Africa	Australia/ Oceania	South America
Croatia	Canada	Czech Republic	Egypt	France
Iraq	Israel		Kenya	New Zealand
South Africa	Switzerland	The United States	The Arctic Ocean	The Pacific Ocean
Antarctica	Europe	Algeria	Austria	People's Republic of China

Around the World Bingo

Democratic Republic of the Congo	England	Germany	India	Italy
Mexico	Poland	South Korea	Syria	Venezuela
The Atlantic Ocean	The Southern Ocean (Antarctic)		Asia	North America
Argentina	Brazil	Colombia	Denmark	Ethiopia
Greece	Ireland	Japan	The Netherlands	The Russian Federation

© Barbara M. Peller

Around the World Bingo

Spain	Turkey	Vietnam	The Indian Ocean	Africa
Australia/ Oceania	South America	Croatia	Austria	People's Republic of China
Democratic Republic of the Congo	England		Germany	India
Ireland	Japan	The Netherlands	The Russian Federation	Switzerland
The United States	The Arctic Ocean	The Pacific Ocean	Antarctica	Europe

Around the World Bingo

Czech Republic	Algeria	Egypt	France	Iraq
India	Italy	Mexico	Poland	Syria
Venezuela	South Korea		The Atlantic Ocean	The Southern (Antarctic) Ocean
North America	Asia	Argentina	Brazil	Colombia
Ethiopia	Denmark	Greece	Ireland	Japan

Around the World Bingo

The Netherlands	The Russian Federation	Spain	Turkey	Japan
The Indian Ocean	Africa	Europe	Argentina	Canada
Democratic Republic of the Congo	Ethiopia		Iraq	Italy
Austria	Syria	South America	Vietnam	Asia
The Netherlands	Colombia	South Africa	The Pacific Ocean	Egypt

Around the World Bingo

The Atlantic Ocean	Germany	Ireland	Kenya	Italy
South Korea	Poland	South Africa	New Zealand	Vietnam
Argentina	The United States		Africa	Europe
The Pacific Ocean	Israel	Brazil	Canada	Egypt
Switzerland	Denmark	Spain	India	Japan

Around the World Bingo: Card No. 11

Around the World Bingo

The Arctic Ocean	The Indian Ocean	The Southern (Antarctic) Ocean	Antarctica	Australia/ Oceania
North America	Algeria	Croatia	Brazil	People's Republic of China
Czech Republic	Denmark		England	France
India	Greece	Israel	Japan	Mexico
New Zealand	The Russian Federation	South Korea	Switzerland	Turkey

Around the World Bingo

The Atlantic Ocean	Venezuela	Vietnam	The Pacific Ocean	Africa
South America	Asia	Austria	Canada	Europe
Argentina	Colombia		Democratic Republic of the Congo	Egypt
Italy	Ethiopia	Turkey	Germany	Iraq
Kenya	Ireland	The Netherlands	Poland	South Africa

Around the World Bingo

The Arctic Ocean	The Atlantic Ocean	Greece	Mexico	Democratic Republic of the Congo
North America	Austria	Italy	The Pacific Ocean	Antarctica
Syria	Germany		Africa	Brazil
The Southern (Arctic) Ocean	Europe	The Russian Federation	Colombia	Kenya
South Korea	Turkey	South Africa	Israel	France

Around the World Bingo

Africa	Antarctica	Europe	Algeria	Croatia
South America	Austria	Canada	People's Republic of China	Czech Republic
Democratic Republic of the Congo	Egypt		England	France
Iraq	Germany	India	Israel	Italy
Kenya	Mexico	New Zealand	Poland	South Africa

Around the World Bingo: Card No. 15

Around the World Bingo

South Korea	Spain	Syria	Turkey	Venezuela
The Atlantic Ocean	Vietnam	The Indian Ocean	North America	The Russian Federation
Argentina	The Pacific Ocean		Asia	Europe
Switzerland	Austria	South America	Canada	Denmark
People's Republic of China	Colombia	The United States	Japan	South Africa

Around the World Bingo

The Pacific Ocean	Vietnam	Poland	Syria	New Zealand
The Russian Federation	Venezuela	The United States	South Africa	Turkey
Switzerland	South Korea		Spain	Mexico
Europe	Kenya	Greece	Japan	Italy
The Netherlands	Israel	Ireland	India	Iraq

Around the World Bingo

The Atlantic Ocean	Germany	France	Ethiopia	Africa
Democratic Republic of the Congo	England	Czech Republic	Mexico	Egypt
Denmark	People's Republic of China		Colombia	Canada
Vietnam	Brazil	Venezuela	Austria	Croatia
The Arctic Ocean	Argentina	North America	The United States	Algeria

Around the World Bingo: Card No. 18

Around the World Bingo

South America	Algeria	Brazil	Canada	Japan
New Zealand	Denmark	Kenya	Germany	England
France	The Russian Federation		Greece	Ireland
Poland	Mexico	South Africa	Turkey	Asia
Argentina	Venezuela	The Indian Ocean	The United States	South Korea

Around the World Bingo: Card No. 19

Around the World Bingo

Asia	Austria	Vietnam	Egypt	Brazil
South Africa	The Southern (Arctic) Ocean	People's Republic of China	Europe	Antarctica
Germany	Australia/ Oceania		India	Kenya
Ethiopia	Denmark	The Netherlands	Poland	France
The United States	Greece	Israel	Mexico	Spain

Around the World Bingo

The Indian Ocean	Africa	Algeria	Croatia	France
Germany	Canada	People's Republic of China	India	Iraq
Ethiopia	Ireland		Denmark	Democratic Republic of the Congo
Mexico	Italy	The Netherlands	Japan	Kenya
New Zealand	Poland	South Africa	Spain	Syria

Around the World Bingo

England	Argentina	Canada	Asia	Ethiopia
The Atlantic Ocean	Denmark	Czech Republic	Iraq	Colombia
Egypt	The Pacific Ocean		Europe	Germany
South Africa	India	South Korea	Japan	Spain
The Russian Federation	Switzerland	Turkey	Venezuela	Africa

Around the World Bingo

The Arctic Ocean	Africa	Antarctica	Algeria	Argentina
Greece	Austria	Iraq	Ireland	Brazil
Canada	Czech Republic		Colombia	Egypt
Israel	Ethiopia	Japan	Denmark	France
The Netherlands	Kenya	New Zealand	The Russian Federation	South Africa

Around the World Bingo

The Atlantic Ocean	Spain	Syria	Argentina	Croatia
Democratic Republic of the Congo	Antarctica	France	Germany	Turkey
Vietnam	Mexico		Venezuela	People's Republic of China
India	Canada	Iraq	Egypt	England
Czech Republic	Israel	Italy	Kenya	New Zealand

Around the World Bingo

The Russian Federation	Poland	Canada	Europe	Egypt
Israel	Denmark	The Indian Ocean	Australia/ Oceania	Colombia
Asia	South Korea		Spain	Syria
Ethiopia	Switzerland	The United States	Vietnam	Algeria
Czech Republic	Croatia	Austria	France	Greece

Around the World Bingo: Card No. 25

Around the World Bingo

Israel	England	Greece	Germany	Ireland
Czech Republic	India	People's Republic of China	The Pacific Ocean	Colombia
Denmark	North America		Egypt	France
Spain	Japan	New Zealand	Kenya	Mexico
The Russian Federation	Poland	South Korea	Switzerland	Turkey

Around the World Bingo

South Korea	Spain	Croatia	Denmark	The Southern (Antarctic) Ocean
North America	Argentina	The United States	The Pacific Ocean	Venezuela
England	South America		Brazil	Canada
Germany	Europe	South Africa	Vietnam	France
Mexico	Italy	Ethiopia	Poland	The Russian Federation

Around the World Bingo

The Indian Ocean	Austria	Brazil	Canada	France
Denmark	Asia	People's Republic of China	South Africa	Africa
India	South Korea		Democratic Republic of the Congo	Greece
Venezuela	Germany	Spain	Switzerland	Japan
Kenya	Iraq	Syria	Israel	Egypt

Around the World Bingo: Card No. 28

© Barbara M. Peller

Around theWorld Bingo

South Korea	Austria	France	Germany	Spain
South Africa	Greece	The Pacific Ocean	North America	Brazil
Europe	Czech Republic		Canada	Denmark
Italy	England	The United States	Ethiopia	Turkey
New Zealand	Switzerland	Asia	The Netherlands	Venezuela

Around the World Bingo: Card No. 29

Around the World Bingo

The Atlantic Ocean	Algeria	Kenya	Vietnam	People's Republic of China
The Russian Federation	Europe	Ireland	The Arctic Ocean	Japan
Spain	South America		Austria	Turkey
The Netherlands	Democratic Republic of the Congo	South Africa	Mexico	Italy
Croatia	Germany	Venezuela	South Korea	New Zealand